Mom, I Choose You

by Danielle A. Bell

Dedication

This book is dedicated to my sons Logan and Orion Campbell. You love me to the moon and back, and I love you even more beyond the stars.

From day one until forever mom, I choose you.
Why? Because you chose me before I even grew.

You nurtured me in your belly,
And you showered me with love,

You provide me with infinite kisses,
And the tightest most bestest hugs.

I know you've lost sleep watching as I rest,
And struggled to stay awake when I play,

You've even dozed off a time or two,
But that's our secret that I won't give away,

You teach me without a sound
Just watching you care for me,

And when the roles reverse with time,
I'll do the same you wait and see.

I could not ask for a better mom,
Or chef or forever best friend,

Or role model, or nurturer, or teacher,
Or bed time buddy when the day ends.

I promise to forever love you,
And make every sacrifice worthwhile,

I promise to turn any tears you've cried,
Into a gums and dimples revealing smile.

Happy
Birthday
mommy

This day is a special day,
And another day to love and choose you,

And for the next 364 days,
I'll be appreciative for all that you do.

Thank You!

Date: ___/___/___

Mom, I Choose You

Date: ___/___/___

Mom, I Choose You

Mom, I Choose You

Date: ___/___/___

Mom, I Choose You

____

____

____

____

____

____

____

Date: ___/___/___

Mom, I Choose You

____

____

____

____

____

____

____

About the Author

Danielle Bell is a mom, a poet, a nurse and now a publisher of children's books! Her book is written from the perspective of a child, whose love for their mom is evident before the child can even speak. Danielle wants all of the moms and caregivers to feel the appreciation and love that they effortlessly and timelessly give from birth to adulthood and beyond. You can look forward to more published material from perspective that is not usually taken. In the meantime, enjoy this token of love and appreciation.... with a little journaling to capture all the reasons why your little one chooses you!